# Let's build a HOUSE

## Mick Manning & Brita Granström

**W**

FRANKLIN WATTS

LONDON • SYDNEY

Let's build a house!
But what sort of house?
There have been so many sorts,
made from so many things...

A house is a warm safe place
to live. We must make sure
we choose the best materials
to build it with.

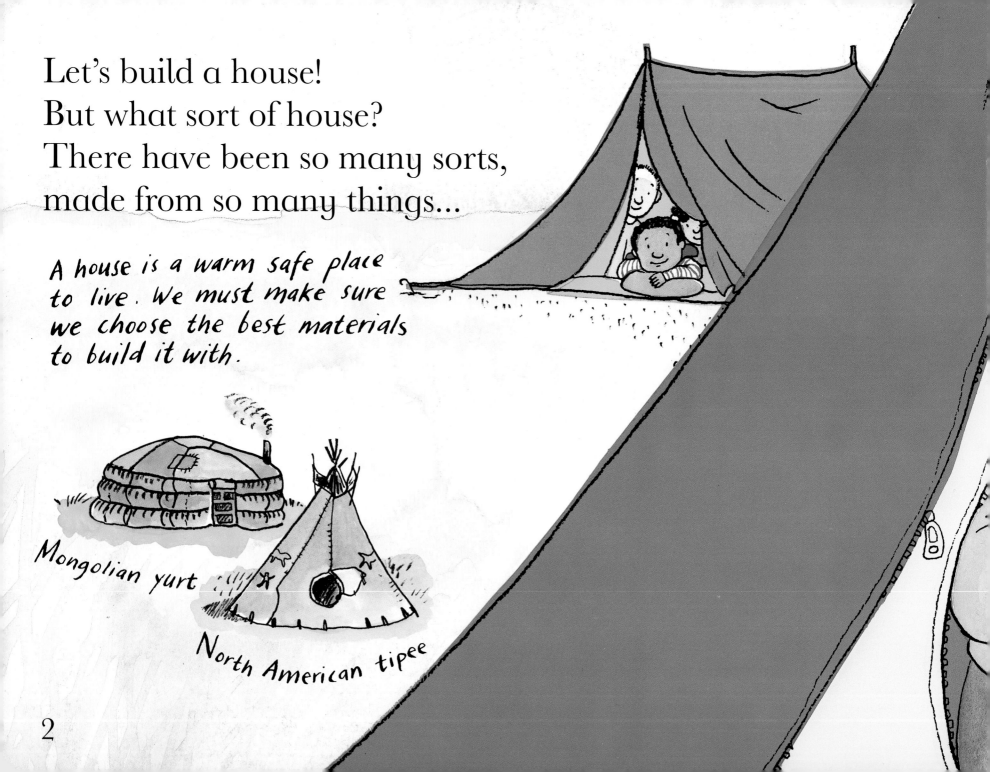

Mongolian yurt

North American tipee

Long ago, tents used to be made from wooden poles with skins stretched across them. Now they are made from metal and waterproof fabric.

3

We could make a cabin of logs, chopped and stacked in a forest clearing – but we'd have to chop down a lot of trees!

Log cabins were houses made by people living near pine forests.

Joints cut like this.

The gaps between the logs were filled with mud, moss or hair to keep out the cold.

5

If it gets really cold and snowy,
we could make an igloo.
We'd be safe in there if polar
bears came a-prowling!

Igloos are built by the Inuit people. They may
be built of blocks of ice but they are warm
and cosy inside.

Ice blocks are laid
in a spiral ...

...the person on the inside has
to cut a way out!

In Sweden, there is a hotel made entirely
of ice - even the beds. It melts in the summer!

7

If the weather was warmer, we could make a hut of mud and sticks. We could give it a thatched roof, woven like a bird's nest!

Mud mixed with straw and plastered on a frame dries strong and hard.

← thatching

Thatched roofs are made from dried reeds.

8

9

How about building a castle?
We'd need to build high stone
walls and fix on a strong wooden
door. Then no one could get in –
unless we let them!

Stone has to be shaped with special tools.

hammer

mallet

chisel

Long ago oxen were used to pull heavy loads.

ox

10

wooden frame

tiles

A castle is huge – what about a little bungalow instead, built from red bricks 'buttered' with cement? Look! I've drawn a plan.

Roofs are a frame of wood usually covered with tiles made of slate, clay or concrete.

Bricks are stuck together with cement called mortar.

13

Let's order a kit house! It all comes on the back of a lorry. 'You can build them in a day,' that's what the magazines say!

Kit houses are delivered pre-built in sections – some are already wallpapered!

Insulation goes under roofs and the spaces inside the wooden walls to stop heat escaping.

Paper screens can be used to divide rooms →

Inside walls can help hold up the roof, others just divide the rooms.

Walls can be made of brick stone, wood or plasterboard.

16

What about inside?
That's important, too.
We need plasterboard
walls to make the rooms.
Underneath the floor,
we can lay wires for
electricity and telephone.

Floorboards are made of soft wood
like pine or spruce. Pine logs are
sliced into floorboards. Floors can
also be made of stone and concrete.

17

We musn't forget a staircase, and then water pipes for the kitchen and bathroom – we could have a shower *and* a bath...

When the wires and pipes are in place it's time for the plasterers to make the wall nice and smooth.

18

A staircase is ready made
of wood or metal.

I'd like a conservatory extension all made of glass – just like a greenhouse. It would be warm and sunny enough to grow tropical flowers and tomatoes.

In many countries windows have two layers of glass to keep out the cold and draughts – it's called double glazing.

20

Concrete is cement with small stones added.

Reinforced concrete is concrete poured around metal rods — it is <u>very</u> strong!

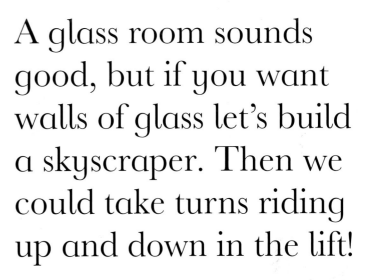

A glass room sounds good, but if you want walls of glass let's build a skyscraper. Then we could take turns riding up and down in the lift!

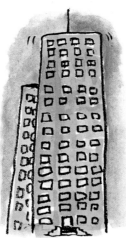

Skyscrapers are made of steel girders, reinforced concrete and strong glass.

They are designed to bend a little in strong winds — so they don't blow down!

The use of steel girders means buildings can be built very high.

steel girders

23

I'd choose to build a little shack on an empty beach. I'd make it from corrugated iron and driftwood, and all sorts of other things left by the tide... And you lot – you could all help!

A shack is one of the simplest houses.

Corrugated metal is a cheap material, used for roofs and walls all over the world. But it gets hot in the sun and is very noisy when it rains!

There are all sorts of homes and all sorts of ways of building them – from log cabins to skyscrapers. If you could build a house, which would you choose?

# How materials are made...

**THATCH**

① Reeds grow by water

② They are cut and dried

③ And stacked in bundles ready for use.

bill hook

**WOOD**

① Wood comes from trees.

② It's cut down

chainsaw

axe

③ And seasoned (dried out)

④ Wood can be cut and sawed easily!

**STONE**

① Stone is quarried out of the ground.

② It's broken up into rough lumps.

③ And 'dressed'— cut into shape with a chisel.

mallet

chisel

28

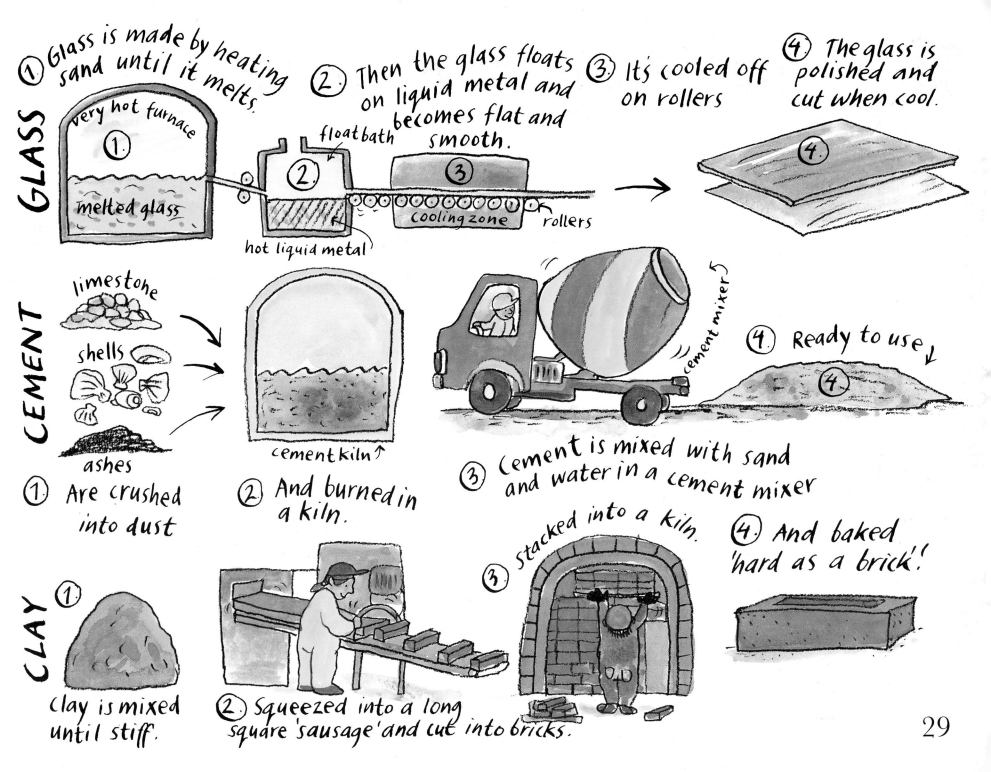

**GLASS**

① Glass is made by heating sand until it melts.

② Then the glass floats on liquid metal and becomes flat and smooth.

③ It's cooled off on rollers

④ The glass is polished and cut when cool.

very hot furnace
① melted glass

float bath
②
hot liquid metal

③ Cooling zone
rollers

④

**CEMENT**

limestone

shells

ashes

① Are crushed into dust

② And burned in a kiln.
cement kiln ↑

cement mixer

③ Cement is mixed with sand and water in a cement mixer

④ Ready to use ↓
④

**CLAY**

① clay is mixed until stiff.

② Squeezed into a long square 'sausage' and cut into bricks.

③ Stacked into a kiln.

④ And baked 'hard as a brick'!

29

# Helpful words

**Bungalow** is the name given to a house with only one floor – there is no upstairs (pages 12, 13).

**Cement** is a fine powder made from limestone. Mixed with sand and water, it sets hard like stone. It can be used to 'glue' bricks together (pages 12, 13).

**Concrete** is made from cement with small stones added. It is much stronger than cement and can be used to make bricks and walls. Reinforced concrete is concrete poured around metal rods. It is strongest of all and can be used to build bridges and skyscrapers (pages 22, 23).

**Corrugated iron** is sheets of iron metal bent into wavy ridges, which makes it stronger than if it was just flat. Plastic and other materials can also be corrugated (page 25).

**Extension** is the name we give to an extra part of a house added on later, after the rest of the house has been built (page 20).

**Insulation** is a way of stopping heat escaping from houses. Insulation can be made of fibres or foam put inside walls and under the roof (page 14).

**Inuit** is the name given to people who live in the Arctic, particularly in Greenland and North America (pages 6, 7).

**Joints** are the places where two pieces of wood are joined together (pages 4, 5).

**Plaster** is a paste coated on walls to make them smooth. It sets hard when it dries. Plaster is made from a mixture of lime and cement (page 18).

**Plasterboard** is board made of paper or fibre covered with plaster. It is used for walls inside houses (pages 16, 17).

**Thatch** is a roofing material made from bundles of dry reeds, grass or straw (pages 8, 9).

**Tipees** are tents that some Native Americans used to make for their homes (page 2).

**Yurts** are the tents of the Mongol people from north-east Asia. Many Mongols are nomads who do not live in one place, but move around the huge grasslands that they live in (page 2).

**For Melker Granström with love**

This edition 2014

First published by Franklin Watts,
338 Euston Road, London NW1 3BH

Franklin Watts Australia,
Level 17 / 207 Kent Street, Sydney NSW 2000

Text and illustrations © 1999 Mick Manning and Brita Granström
Notes and activities © 2005, 2014 Franklin Watts

The illustrations in this book were made by Brita and Mick.
Find out more about Mick and Brita at www.mickandbrita.com

Series editor: Rachel Cooke
Art Director: Robert Walster

A CIP catalogue record is available from the British Library.
Dewey Classification 690

Printed in China

ISBN 978 1 4451 2899 3

Franklin Watts is a division of Hachette Children's Books,
an Hachette UK company. www.hachette.co.uk